POTTER HE.⌣.⼁⼂⼂

THE HEART OF BROADLAND

THE BRIDGE

The low narrow round arch of the ancient bridge at Potter Heigham spans the river Thurne, making a bottle neck for the holiday boats. Traffic lights hold up the cars, wide vehicles scrape its parapets and there have been many near misses by pedestrians. On one occasion a young man, certain he was going to be trapped between a bus and the wall dived over into the river. Wet and indignant he scrambled to the bank and made some forthright remarks about the bridge and buses in general.

Bridge and ducks.   Photo: Bert High

In 1940 Arthur Mee wrote *'All the world knows its old bridge. . . some of its grey stone may have been here in the days of King John. In summer it is gay with the spirit of holiday, and the yachts and wherries draw up to it for the night. There are windmills round about, and old thatched cottages and new red roofs are in the lanes leading to the lovely old village church.'*

When the river is high it is impossible for large craft to pass beneath, sometimes those who have ventured to Hickling cannot return, and many boats bear scars from close shaves. It requires such careful navigation that a pilot is there to take hire craft through. In the old days masters of wherries often had to pile on ballast of stones, sinking their wherries dangerously low, and use jacks to force their craft through. In the late 1940s the newly appointed Vicar, Reverend B Goodwin, was persuaded to lower himself from the bridge parapet on to a cruiser in difficulty, adding his thirteen and a half stone to help the vessel through.

Church Road circa 1923.

View from bridge circa 1902.

Looking towards the bridge from Repps, 1920s.

It is listed as a fine, narrow stone bridge and some say it was built in 1385, possibly by monks from St Benet's. It remains mainly medieval in construction and consists of a large segmental arch, flanked by small triangular arches, with moulded heads and chamfered ribs, buttresses and cutwaters. The brick parapet dates from the 17th or 18th century. The bypass saved the bridge from demolition, but the problems it causes remain a subject of controversy.

Alan and Sonny Amis, out in a motor boat, dashed to rescue the driver! (Photo: Eastern Daily Press)

THE NAME

There have been several variations on the name of the place we now call Potter Heigham. At Domesday it was written as Echam and was *'held by Godric of Hecham'*; it was very small, listed as having two freemen, two acres and was valued at 2d. About 1160 it became Hecham. Soon after that the prefix *'Potter'* was added, relating to the Medieval industry. In 1182 it was Hegham Pottere and in 1254 Potteres Hecham.

The site of the pottery is north of Decoy Lane on the boundary with Catfield, part of a large field known as *'Pothills'*. Fragments of pottery have been recovered from this site and identified as being from a late

Medieval kiln. The site has not been excavated and there may be earlier kilns in the same area.

It has been suggested that the pottery industry began in Roman times, but the archaeological evidence at present available (just a few scraps of sherds held in the Castle Museum in Norwich) suggests the pottery is post Roman. It is believed to have been working until the 15th century, and mounds of broken pottery and ash were flattened in the 19th century.

In the Register of the Abbey of St Benet's (to which at one time the village belonged) it was listed as Hecham juxta Ludham to distinguish it from Hecham juxta Norwicum, necessary because the Abbey owned land in both parishes. This meant that all people in the village were feudal tenants of the Benedictine Abbey of St Benet's at Holme, which had manors and lands that filled eleven pages of Domesday book, and stretched over a radius of 25 miles.

A slight hitch as the new village sign is unveiled, 1981. (Photo: Ivan Gould)

The medieval records of St Benet's Abbey record vast sales of peat from its parishes, and it is known that by the end of the 12th century the Abbey had acquired rights in turbary in Potter Heigham, although these were probably in existence long before then. Turf digging was probably a seasonal operation undertaken during the summer months, and must have demanded constant attention to drainage. Turf cutting continued until the industry declined in the 14th and 15th centuries. Flooding in late medieval times created Hickling Broad, including that part of it which lies in Potter Heigham. By the 16th century most Broads were in existence roughly as we know them today.

THE PEASANT'S REVOLT

Potter Heigham people were among those who were stirred to rebellion, being dissatisfied with their lowly status. As serfs, subsisting by agriculture, they had to render compulsory service to the landed classes. This work increased greatly in the years following the Black Death, which had caused a labour shortage. No doubt they had also heard the preaching of the Lollards on the equality of man, and as if that was not enough, the Poll Tax had been imposed, at 4d per head.

On the night of 23rd June 1381 there was a rumour that Bishop Despenser was at the Abbey. The peasants had heard that he intended to crush the rebellion, so about 400 people from Ludham and Potter Heigham, armed with sticks and cudgels and led by William de Kimberley, the Abbot's carter, went down the causeway in the night. Their intention was to attack the Abbey and capture or kill the Bishop.

Unfortunately for the rebels the monks were always up and at prayer by two am and were thus able to defend the Abbey from attack, especially as it was surrounded by the massive walls and gateway, built only 30 years previously. It has been estimated that there were then about 24 monks, another 75 or so servants, and many guests and refugee monks who had fled from other monasteries, making in all about 200 people within its walls. They managed to resist the attack.

The rumour was found to have been false, for Bishop Despenser was not at St Benet's that night. The peasants withdrew the following morning, and there is no account of casualties. Most of them probably returned to their lands, but some men of Potter Heigham, Ludham, Thurne and Ashby walked northwards towards North Walsham. There Bishop Despenser defeated them in a skirmish, and folk memory insists that bodies were buried at the site of the battle.

CIVIL WAR

Little is known of what actually happened in Potter Heigham during the Civil War of 1642 to 1646, but that would have been the period when the followers of Cromwell defaced the paintings on the Screen of the church. Most of Norfolk supported the Parliamentarians, but it would appear that the vicar was on the side of the king. A marble wall tablet in the church has the following inscription: *'In memory of Robert Myhil, clerk, vicar, who built the vicarage house, and suffered much in the Oliverian times, for his loyalty, for his piety, charity and sufferings, was beloved in his country and died 22.2.1663. He was appointed in 1626.'*

The church, 1948 (Photo: Betty Gallaugher)

POTTER HEIGHAM IN THE 19TH CENTURY

In common with all Norfolk villages the population grew during the first half of the 19th century. In 1801 there were 58 houses and a population of 321 people. 50 years later the number of houses had more than doubled to 97 and the population increased to 477. After that although the number of houses increased slightly the population declined, and by 1901, 426 people lived in 103 dwellings. The Tithe Map of 1841 shows that the parish had 1140 acres of marshland, 882 acres of old arable land, and 193 acres of land covered by water.

THE VILLAGE SCHOOLS

The first School (almost opposite the present one) was built 1844, with adjoining teacher's house, and became a Board School in 1871. It could accommodate 86 children-but until education became free and compulsory in 1891, getting the children to school was a continual problem. The Log Book which commences on 11th May 1874 was totally preoccupied with attendance, 30 to 40 being about average, although there were about a 100 children in the village.

In June and July many of the boys missed school because they were 'engaged in the Hay', and by the end of that month children were working in the harvest fields, or carrying dinners to their parents.

Poor attendance was often caused by illness, whooping-cough, scarlet fever, diphtheria, influenza, measles or mumps. Another reason was bad weather, and the dreadful state of the roads in wet as well as in snowy weather. Boots were not always waterproof and the girl's long skirts could become bedraggled in the mud. The attendance officer complained that he was unable to compel the children. The board assured the Mistress that *'every pains were taken to teach the mothers ... to see the importance of regular attendance of their children, but that very little attention has been paid to them.'*

The Mistresses constantly resigned. Each new one wrote in the Log book of her arrival, seemingly with high hopes, but these were soon dashed and within a couple of years or so, she would resign. *'Some children were absent for more than a month at a time,'* wrote one. Other entries said -

1877 June 1. *Very thin attendance this week, doubtless owing to it being the fair week.*
1878 Mar 5. *There being sports going on in the village only eight children attended the school so the Mistress gave a half holiday.*
Mar 12. *The children were treated with a bun and an orange each by Mrs French Snr as it was the birthday of Miss Mary French, (daughter of the vicar) and the Mistress gave a half holiday.*
May 10. *The children were treated after school this morning with buns, sweets, nuts etc by Mrs French Snr in honour of Master W D French's birthday and the mistress gave a half holiday.*
The Rev French is noted occasionally as *'looking in at the school for a few minutes.'*

The school in 1928, in charge of Miss Thirza Bond, Miss Sophie Wilson and Miss Kate Little. (Photo: Betty Gallaugher)

1878 Nov 12. Flooding *'rendered the school inaccessible.'* It was closed *'till the waters abated'* and reopened on Nov 25th.

1880 Jan 15. *The school reopened this day, only one pupil attended in the morning and three in the afternoon.*

Next day there were six. A list of absentees was sent to the Board. By Feb 25th numbers had risen to 25. Attendance remained low all year.

In September the Inspector reported *'The School is in a poor condition. Attendance is miserably irregular and the results of Examination very poor. The Infant class is the best in the school. The room needs alteration and the unused class-room should be repaired and used. More books should be provided.'* The Mistress complained that the house was damp and in poor condition.

Throughout the 1880s the average attendance was about 50 to 70 children. Then on Sept 28th 1891, Henry Hardwicke the Headmaster wrote- *'Reopened school after recess. Free education having been adopted by the board, no fees were paid by the scholars this morning. Attendance was excellent - 103 children.'* By 1892 the average attendance far exceeded the accommodation provided. Plans were drawn up for a new school and house, these were built in 1894 and the new school was opened on 17th September with an attendance of 106 children. Only one child was absent with scarlet fever.

The last report from the old school said *"Notwithstanding the overcrowded state of the rooms, the children were in very good order and passed a very creditable exam, both in Elementary and Class subjects. The arithmetic, for neatness, accuracy and intelligence deserves special mention. . .'*

1895 May 6 Mr Frederick Goldsmith and his wife took charge of the school. They intended to remain only for a year or two, but stayed for the rest of their lives, and for thirty years were the teachers.

There were still some difficulties with attendance, Mr Goldsmith wrote of parents who complained about their children being kept in till half past one. One such boy ran off. *'On returning this afternoon, he pleaded his mother told him he was not to be kept in. I told him he would have to be punished. He refused to take the punishment so, as his words and manner had been very impudent from the first I laid him across the desk and gave him five or six strokes with stick across the buttocks. The mother paid me a visit after school but when I explained the matter to her she became very tractable. After objurgating the gentleman she disrespectfully termed 'Old look-'em up' she told me I ought to have given her boy the stick yesterday for being late, and then went home apparently well satisfied.'*

The school punishment book starts on 18th July 1900 and indicates how common was the use of the cane in those days. The first entries related to two girls and one boy who were each caned one stroke on the hand, for *'gross carelessness and disobedience, bad work and laziness, slovenly paper followed by copying.'* The following day Ivy Simmons was given one stroke for continual talking.

The September 1900 term started with five boys each receiving two strokes for hooliganism on leaving school the previous night. Another ten were caned during that month. One boy was caned twice in one afternoon for being lazy, talkative, having dirty hands, and taking all afternoon to finish drawing.

Other offences which merited corporal punishment included: pulling girls' hair; being absent without excuse; punching another boy's head; disorder; not staying late; continual talking and neglect of work; disorderliness and inattention (one of the most common offences); stone throwing; falsehood; chalking on walls; rowdy rude shouting; malicious damage to books or pens; bringing nuts for eating in school: writing dirty words on gate; bad behaviour going home. One naughty girl peppered the flowers!

Punishment varied. One stroke on one hand was the most common, but it graduated upwards; one stroke on each hand, two strokes on one hand, two strokes on arm, two light strokes on the buttocks. 'For getting up a fight on leaving school as had been cautioned against overnight, gave several boys three or four strokes on shoulders.'

The years go by and the same names, even the same families fill the files of the punishment book. Obviously they never learned. The children get no better behaved despite the use of the cane. That is just the way life was then.

DECOY

Although the existence of the Decoy is before living memory, the road so-named today must have led to the working area of wildfowlers from the village. Even today it is a solitary place, on the far fringe of the parish, winding towards the enchanting wilderness of the broad. One can easily imagine that a 100 years ago it would have been an ideal spot for this method of luring down a good *'bag'* of wild ducks.

Decoys were made by erecting a curving line of semicircular hoops over a specially dug channel, about 70 or 80 yards in length. The first hoop was about ten feet high, the next a little smaller, each one diminished in size until the last hoop was only about two or three feet high. The water also became shallower and narrower. The line of hoops, called the decoy pipe, was covered with wire netting, leaving the mouth open.

Tame ducks were kept in the area, on a grassy bank near the open water and were always fed just inside the pipe, their presence acting as a lure to wild duck. The wildfowler watched in his boat, in a *'hide'* of rushes and when a good number of wild duck had congregated he sent his dog, usually a little fox terrier, along to scare all the ducks into the water. The tame ducks would swim into the mouth of the decoy and the well trained terrier plunge into the water and encourage the wild ducks forward until they too were inside the mouth of the pipe which was so large they were unaware of it.

The man in his boat then came out. The frightened ducks would try to fly away, but could only go further into the ever narrowing decoy pipe until they were trapped. The fowler wrung the necks of the wild ducks and put them into his basket to sell. The tame ones were returned to the grassy patch to lure down more victims. Up to a 100 birds have been caught in one *'push'*.

Decoying and shooting on the marshes and broad had been considered a traditional right by local marshmen from time immemorial, but the modern world was beginning to encroach on village life. Some people were alarmed that, with the ease of transport since the coming of the railway, too many wildfowl and fish were being caught and sent away to London. Also there were visitors who would pay well for shooting rights, and the activities of the local men was detrimental to their sport. Potter Heigham men argued that they had a right of access because the waters were tidal. Some went to London to give evidence in a long remembered court case, but out of their natural element, barely educated and unable to state their case adequately, they were defeated.

DRAINAGE MILL.

The drainage mill was operated by the Grapes family from early in the 19th century and for a decade or so into the 20th. A tallish tower windpump, built of brick, it makes a landmark from both river and road. It was working until about 1938, latterly with the assistance of a steam pump. Mills tend to take the name of the man who operates them, so soon after Harold High moved into the Millhouse in 1924 the mill assumed its present name, and as the High brothers were the last to operate it, it has continued to be called High's Mill. He was employed by the Smallburgh Internal Drainage Board to attend to the drainage and keep the dykes in good order. His income was augmented by using the land around the millhouse as a market garden and he kept a herd of cows on the marsh.

Aerial view of High's Mill, with house and smallholding. (Photo: Bert High)

The aerial photograph taken about 1960, shows from left to right, the mill, the cowshed, the house, and on the far right straddling the dyke, the electric pump. The other small building was to store the coal which was brought up by wherry to feed the steam pump; this had been installed at the end of the 19th century. It had a big chimney and was housed in another building, pulled down in 1945. When there was heavy rain coupled with a high tide the windmill was able only to *'cream off'* only the top of the water, it could not pump enough to keep the marshes properly drained. Then the steam pump had to be brought into action and it ruled Mr High's life. It took an hour to get up enough steam to start pumping and all the time it was working he had to be continuously vigilant, watching temperature gauges, oiling the open bearings, carting and shovelling coal to feed the hungry boiler. He dared not leave it even to get a cup of tea, so his wife took it over to him, and if he was pumping water at night he would stay there all night.

The Horsey flood of 1938 ended the tyranny of the steam pump. Sea water covered the marshes and as it was pumped off through the big old boiler the salt caused such corrosion that the boiler had to be replaced. An electric pump was then installed, using the same turbine, and that proved to be so efficient and economical it took the place not only of the steam pump but of the old windpump as well.

13

The duty of the Drainage Board's employee at the mill included keeping the dykes clean. This work was called dyke drawing, and was done manually every year. Bert High, who took over from his brother in 1945, explains the process. The dyke and its edges would be *'all grown up, and first you go along with a scythe and trim an area as close as you can to the water, then you go along with another scythe which is bent backwards slightly, cutting the weeds under the water at the edge of the dyke, Finally with another smaller implement on a long handle, called a 'mag' you cut the weeds in the middle of the dyke and if you were lucky you can pull most of the weeds out as you went along and shake them on to the bank.'*

He recalls some memorable winters, especially in 1947, when after the birth of his daughter in January, they were snowed in and it was ten weeks before he and his wife could get to church for the traditional thanksgiving service. Again in January 1963 for three or four weeks he delivered milk to the Thurne bungalows by biking up and down the river. Later that year he moved into Rose Farm and the millhouse remained unoccupied for many years.

Around that time the mill was sold to Mr William Cooper, who set about repairs to the tower and converted it into a dwelling. Over the years the sails broke and blew down, and in 1939 it was bought by Mr T F Suttle. Half the cap boards were lost in a gale in 1973, and a couple of years later the remains of the sails and fan frame were removed and the cap repaired.

EEL-BOAT

In his book Norfolk Broads and Rivers (1883) G C Davies wrote of *'passing a farmhouse bowered in the trees, a windmill, and a group of peasants exquisitely mirrored in the calm water.'* He was close to Potter Heigham. They stopped for the night near an eel-set, which fascinated him. *'Eel-boats are like the Noah's arks of childhood, and are of ancient appearance; we have never seen a new one. The tarred nets, which are hung up to dry upon stakes around the dyke in which the boat is moored, are carefully kept and well mended. Through the night the eel-fisher sits in his cabin, like some great spider in his web, waiting for the eels the stream will bring to his net.'*

Just such an eel-fisher was Martin Brown. Russell Wright said *'The first time I saw him lying in his hut beside Candle Dyke,I thought he was dead. He'd been drinking. After that I went to work for him. He had two nets, one out and one in, they had to be tarred every so often and they'd get right stiff.'* The season starts in July or August, when the eels with the urge to breed startd to migrate down river, making for the sea. By November the weather is too cold and the eels have mostly gone.

Eel fishermen are almost as mysterious and secretive about their movements as are their prey. Their nets, stretched across the river in lonely places, are vulnerable to damage by boats, or theft. They are held by a stake on either bank, have a heavy chain to keep the bottom down; on top are wooden poles; block and tackle is used to lift them. They are made with three funnels which taper down in such a way that once the eels have passed through they cannot get back. They have to swim further into the ever narrowing net, until finally they are held in the *'poke'* at the end. The net is lowered during the day and lies on the river bed, to allow free passage of boats. At night the eel catcher must stay in his hut and be ready ready to lower the net for any boats on the river. The eels come when the moon is just on the wane, about three nights after the full moon. *'On the first night you'd just get enough for your breakfast,'* said Russell. *'The next night you'd get a little more and the third night should be really good. Once we got 52 stone in one night.'* The biggest eel he caught was 10lbs.'

'We used to get a fair number of eels weighing seven or eight pounds, as big as my arm, and strong; if you didn't get the tail into the bin when you tipped them out of the net, they could flick themselves back into the river. One evening I took some eels to the Royal Oak at Ormesby and accidentally let one out on the floor. It was a tiled floor, smooth and shiny and the eel was wet and slimy. Their tails are immensely strong, and it flipped itself about and the women jumped up on the seats. You couldn't catch it, until someone got a cloth and threw over it. They called me every name under the sun.'

Bert High took over the eel-set from Martin Brown. It was a short distance up river from his house at the mill. Whilst he prepared to snatch what sleep he could in the eel-catcher's hut, his wife walked down the garden path at about 11 pm to check the electric drainage pump. Before she returned to the house and sleeping children, they exchanged flashes of torchlight across the marsh to reassure each other that all was well.

Bert reckoned conditions were perfect when there was a gale blowing the reeds about, and a thunderstorm over Hickling Broad, with rain pelting down and the moon just coming up at about eight o'clock. He recalled with relish one such ideal night. *'That year I thought I was not going to get enough eels to pay my rent. Then suddenly one of these things happened. A gale of wind blew all day and night and again the next day and night.'* He had slept in the hut and in the morning had to let his net down so he could go home and milk his cows. When he went back to empty the net he could hardly believe his luck. *'I got so many* that morning, and I hadn't much time because I had to take my son to the dentist. I just gave up weighing them, untied the 'pouch' from the main net, dragged it alongside the boat back to the hut and tipped them into my keep trunk. I estimate there was a quarter of a ton of eels that morning.' A good haul to send off to Billingsgate fishmarket.

THE CORN MILL

The corn mill at the end of Mill Lane was rebuilt in 1849 by Samuel Boyce, who became the miller in 1836. It remained in that family until 1889, and even after that William Boyce was mill manager. As long ago as 1806 there was a mill on the same site, and even at that date it was described as 'old established' An auction catalogue of the early 19th century described it as 'An excellent POST MILL . . . with a roundhouse and substantial brick and tiled dwelling house, barn, stable, cart sheds and other convenient buildings and piece of land containing altogether about one acre. . . It is well situated for wind, stands within three furlongs of the navigable river from Yarmouth and will manufacture about six lasts per week.'

The corn mill, 1950. (Photo: Clifford Temple)

In 1900 the mill and its house were again put up for auction. By then it was steam powered, and occupied by Mr Moore. It had *'recently been fitted with all the most improved and costly Machinery, including a Ransomes ten hp Semi-Portable Engine with Pump attached, Wheat Cleaner and Revolving Cylinder, Sack Tackle and Hoist Chain, two pairs of French Burr Stones, Flour Mixer, Scalper, Flour Centrifugal, and Oat Crusher'* It was withdrawn at £495.

Subsequently it was bought by Edward Bristow, but he went off to America in 1910. Reba Bristow, who also ran Great Ormesby tower mill, took it over in 1908 and was joined by Alfred in 1912. Reba went away to the war in 1917 and was one of those who never returned. In 1919 the mill was sold to John Blaxell. It became electric in the early 1930s and by then had only one pair of sails and no fan. Milling continued until 1949, and many villagers remember going there for freshly ground flour and chicken feed.

RAILWAY

Work by the Midland and Great Northern Joint Railway that brought modern transport to Potter Heigham began on 15th January 1877 at Yarmouth. By the 7th August the first section via Caister to Ormesby was completed and opened. The next section took the line to Hemsby and Martham and soon six trains a day were running from there to Yarmouth.

Potter Heigham station, looking west, 1898. (Photo: Ronald H Clark)

The five and a half miles to Catfield via Potter Heigham was more difficult to construct because of crossing the river Thurne. The Act of Parliament stipulated that the bridge must be nine feet six inches above 'high water' and have a span of at least 40 feet over the river. The bridge was designed with three 79 feet spans and its main girders were divided into five equal bays. It crossed the river at the same place as the A149 and the line through Potter Heigham to Catfield was opened on 17th January 1880.

The station stood at the junction of Station Road and the A149, just in front of the shop. For seventy-nine years trains puffed and steamed along the line and immediately they made impact upon life in the village. Until then transport had been only by horse-drawn wagons, carts and carriages, or by sailing craft along the river, and cattle, sheep and other animals had all been herded along the roads to market. Soon all the corn and much of the coal and other goods were transported by railway, instead of by wherry. Better transport allowed more perishable crops to be grown such as flowers and fruit, especially raspberries and blackcurrants. The eel catchers and wildfowlers also discovered the value of quick access to the lucrative London markets.

Soon the line was completed through Stalham to North Walsham and way beyond to link up with lines from the Midlands and London. Holiday-makers stepped off the trains, eager to explore the wilds of Norfolk about which they had read in books by such writers as Davies and Suffling. The whole country was suddenly within easy reach of Potter Heigham.

The various railway lines competed to provide good a service to the Norfolk coast and broads. The fastest trains took three hours between Liverpool Street and Cromer with stops at Ipswich and North Walsham, but the Midland and Great Northern had an advantage because many Londoners found Kings Cross more accessible than Liverpool Street. Passengers bound for Potter Heigham could join the connecting train on the same platform at Melton Constable, instead of changing from one station to another at North Walsham. Of equal importance was the contact the trains made with the Midlands. Visitors came from Leicester, Birmingham, Nottingham, Derby, Sheffield, and connections could easily be made to Manchester, Spalding and Melton Mowbray. Special 'boating and fishing' tickets were advertised to tempt holiday-makers to Norfolk.

Well before the First World War, excursions linked with day trips on the Broads, were run from Yarmouth, Sheringham and Cromer to Potter Heigham and other stations near the rivers. Similar outings were relaunched in 1927. By then bus services had been set up in

Charlie and Hannah Bensley on a day trip to Great Yarmouth, 1910. (Photo: Russell Wright)
Class 4MT 2-6-0 with passenger train about to enter Potter Heigham station, viewed from the carriage window. A 4MT 2-6-0 with freight train for Yarmouth waits in the station. Mid 1950.s) (Photo: Dr I Allen. Courtesy M and GN Circle)

competition. Holiday Camps were established at Caister in 1906 and Hemsby in 1933, and it was partly to serve their visitors that miniature halts were opened in the summer of 1933. One of these halts was beside Potter Heigham railway bridge, close to the yachts and riverside bungalows. It was a simple platform, only slightly above rail level, built mainly of sleepers, on which were two seats. The halts operated only in the summer and were served by a steam rail car known as the *'Tantivy'*. This steam powered coach had a fireman and a driver, went to and fro, push-pull, and could carry about 50 passengers.

In August 1912 the river flooded exceptionally badly, covering the line with a great stretch of water It disrupted services for several days and occurred just at the peak period both for summer holiday traffic, and the fruit-growers.

The track was single line, and trains had to be crossed over at certain points by the stations. Main line trains were pulled by handsome yellow engines, and had varnished teak six-wheeled coaches. At that time they were as much a part of the local scene as the church tower, the windmills or the black sails of the wherries. The M and GN, often known as the Muddle and Go Nowhere, is now nostalgically called the Missed and Greatly Needed. It was closed in 1959, and only ten years later the new road was opened, allowing motor traffic to bypass the old *'infamous bridge with its traffic lights and single carriageway.'* It was hailed as a historic day, *'the first road to be built on a railway in this country.'*

FIRST WORLD WAR

In 1915 to 1916 the Gordon Highlanders and the Cameronians set up a camp in the fields on which St Nicholas Way and the Thoroughfare have been built. The footpath, which led from Station Road to Dovehouse Lane was closed and roadways, canteens and guardroom were built. A sentry stood guard to challenge villagers who passed by.

Billy Durrant recalled *'When I was a boy I'd rush out on a Sunday morning and sit on the wall at Bethel Farm to see the soldiers march by on church parade. I loved to watch them, with kilts swinging and bagpipes playing. They often used to stand up by the church to practise the pipes too. I've always liked bagpipes since then. They were here for about six months before they went off to France. The soldiers were good to us boys, I really missed them when they left.'* After the Scots regiment some cavalry came, with horses and mules, training with gun carriages, but it was the Scottish infantry that was especially remembered.

CHILDHOOD

'You could whip a top all the way to school, from anywhere in the village.' Or run a hoop; iron hoops were made by the blacksmith and bowled along with a stick. Games followed in season, skipping, marbles, balls, rhyming chants. There was no traffic, but morning and evening you would meet a herd of cows being being brought up from the marsh for milking, or taken back afterwards.

A familiar scene in the 1940s. Cows in the pond, Church Road. (Photo: Ronnie George)

Looking towards Marsh Road, 1950. (Photo: Clifford Temple)

In springtime, after school, some boys were sent to the fields bird-scaring. They stayed there till dusk, threw stones at the crows, and shouted to frighten them off the corn. They got very little money for it. Sometimes they took bird's eggs and sold them to visitors, it was not illegal then. There were high hedges along the lanes, wild flowers grew on the banks and in the plantations. Primroses were so plentiful that children would pick baskets full to be tied into bunches for sale at Yarmouth market. Violets, both white and blue, scented the lanes, and down Mill Road, on the *'hover'* wild orchids, bright carmine spikes, sprang up every summer.

The old word *'hover'* is a link with the past, pronounced as in *'hoverfly'* and meaning turf dug for burning. Suffling, writing in *'Land of the Broads'* in 1887 says *'peat, or as it is here called 'hovers', is when properly dried, a capital and economical substitute for coal. It gives off a blue smoke when burning, and this, as it rises from the cottars chimneys, wafts a rather pleasant perfume in the air, which is a great improvement on the soot-laden, evil-smelling smoke of the metropolis. A peat-ground, properly managed, is a rather valuable holding . . . The peat blocks, when cut, are about four inches square (shrinking by drying to about three and a quarter inches) by from two feet to two and a half feet long (the depth of the boggy surface soil). Each square foot, therefore produces nine 'hovers' . . . these are retailed at from 1s to 1s 6d per 100.'*

The children who lived in Decoy enjoyed playing in the old *'clay allotment'*. This was a relic from the days when it was the duty of each village to keep its own roads in order. The clay and gravel extracted from the Surveyor's Allotment was used to mend potholes. One man was appointed to oversee the work. Unpaid, having to commandeer men and carts from the farmers, it was an unenviable position that was held for a year or so and thankfully passed on.

So much fruit was grown that the school closed for three weeks in July, to allow the children to help with the picking, mostly of blackcurrants and raspberries. Useful not only for the growers, but also for the many families who relied on the extra money to buy winter coats and boots. After the picking school reopened for a couple of weeks, then broke up for another three weeks holiday whilst the harvest was gathered in. Again the older children were heavily involved, either working in the fields with their parents, leading the horses, or carrying hot dinners to the men in the fields. The work went on from 6 am until 9 pm or later, cutting the corn, standing it in 'shocks', loading and carting it to the farms, stacking and thatching the stacks. At the end of harvest a family might get an extra £7 or £8 with which to go to Yarmouth and fit themselves out with essential new clothes to last the coming year.

Once a year the children rode merrily away on their Sunday School outing. Farmers loaned wagons, each pulled by a couple of horses, turned out with pride, superbly groomed by the teamsmen, harness gleaming and brass jingling. Straw was spread over the bottom of the wagon for the children to sit on, adult helpers perched on benches, and off they trundled to Winterton, Sea Palling or Hemsby for a day at the seaside.

Chapel Anniversaries, on Whitsundays, were held in Dove Barn. On the day before it had to be cleaned and decorated with greenery and lilac (almost every cottage had a lilac tree). The chapel organ was carted into the barn and heaved on to a trestle stage. Benches were set along the walls, and some of the little girls were afraid to lean back in case they messed up their best dresses. They had been rehearsing for six weeks or more, ready to stand up say their *'pieces'*. There was never enough seating for all, and in fine weather some spilled outside. A collection was made for the Sunday School.

Dove Barn, scene of
Methodist Anniversaries.
(Photo: Clifford Temple)

Stalham Town Band, 1950. (Photo: Clifford Temple)

Upbringing was strict, both at school and at home. *'We were never allowed out. I daren't ask to go out in the evening except to go to Christian Endeavour. My parents never let me read the newspapers. We wore children's clothes until we left school, never allowed to look grown-up before that.'* Thursday evening at Christian Endeavour was eagerly looked forward to. It was the only place the boys and girls could meet together, outside school.

Canon Meadows-White is specially remembered. He wore a big brimmed black hat, and rode a tricycle. It often stood outside the cottages, whilst he was visiting. One day several children tried to ride it but they only succeeded in turning it over. They were terrified and ran away fast.

THE REGATTA

The first Thursday in August was the Regatta, a date to be relished, when it seemed as if everybody for miles around gathered in the vicinity of the old bridge. Rhubarb Underwood's fun fair had already set up its colourful collection of rides, dodg'ems, cakewalk, coconut shies, boxing booth and other stalls in front of the Bridge Hotel, and spilled over to the Potter Heigham side. Yachts milled around in the narrow river, jostling for good starting positions. Wherries were moored along the river bank in front of Herbert Woods' Yacht Station, from which officials fired the starting guns for the races. There were swimming races too, and a greasy pole projecting over the river on which young men, armed with well stuffed pillows, jousted to knock each other into the water. For the children sports were organised on the marsh beyond the bridge.

All day the policeman struggled to keep the bridge clear enough to allow the traffic to pass over - there was no alternative route, horses and carts, cars, lorries or buses could move only at snail's pace among the thronging crowds. The pubs were open all day, until midnight, and well patronised. In the evening the fair came into its own with flaring lights and merry organ music, and as night fell the event finished with a grand firework display that lit the skies over the marshes, and threw up stars that were reflected in the slow flowing river.

The Regatta, 1957. (Photo Eastern Daily Press)

Bridge Hotel, 1930.

WORK

On leaving school the girls went into service; there was no other work for them. Several went to Yarmouth, or became domestic servants in the village boarding houses that catered for the growing holiday trade. The vicarage at Potter Heigham always had two maids living in, and so did the bigger farmers. Most girls were allowed one half day off a week and on that evening had to be in by half past nine. They wore print dresses in the mornings and black with cap and apron in the afternoons, and were expected to say *'sir'* or *'madam'* when spoken to.

The general routine was to be up at 6.30 every morning to blacklead the grates and light the fires. Downstairs rooms had to be swept and dusted. Sometimes trays of early morning tea had to be taken up. At eight o'clock there would be a break for breakfast, after which two girls together would start on the bedrooms. In addition to making the beds, sweeping and dusting the bedrooms, slops had to be emptied, and the washstand cleaned, ewers and carafes refilled. The trays from morning tea were carried down and crockery washed up. It was then time to change into afternoon uniform ready for lunch at one o'clock. Some had to wait at table. In the afternoons there was silver and brass to be cleaned, and the lamps trimmed. After tea in winter fires had to be lit in bedrooms, cans of hot water carried up and later more slops to be emptied. Before retiring to bed the trays for the following morning were laid out.

A washerwoman went in to do washing, for which there was a huge copper in the scullery. The housemaid's own washing was taken home for her mother to do, caps and aprons boiled in the copper in their own outhouse. The box iron was then in use, with heaters put into the fire, lifted out with tongs when red hot and dropped into the iron box. It was easier when the more modern type was introduced and was stood in front of the fire to heat.

Young men often cycled around from village to village, *'girl hunting,'* one elderly lady smiled mischievously, recalling her first meeting with her own husband. Records suggest that in previous centuries the young men and women habitually walked to Catfield, Ludham, Hickling, Sea Palling and even Winterton, meeting up with other young people, getting together, and when the time was right, meeting their future spouses. In this century it was much the same, only they moved rather more freely on bikes.

When the boys left school they worked on the farms, often following their fathers on to the same farms, and the same trades becoming teamsmen, or herdsmen. In Potter Heigham there was also a close link with the sea. Mr Balls of Rookery Farm had a herring fleet as well as being a farmer, and even before he came to the village many men and boys went to sea on the trawlers. For some it was seasonal, following the herring in the autumn, returning home on Saturday afternoons and off to sea again on Sunday evenings. Others went out on the drifters and were away for three months at a time, returning home for about two weeks whilst the boat had a refit.

Eric Thain, whose father and grandfather were both watermen, worked on his father's wherries when he first left school. The family had four wherries, berthed in front of the Bridge Hotel. In the winter they transported sugar beet to Cantley. A huge quantity of beet was carted to the staithe by cart or lorry and piled up there in readiness for the right tide. Two men from the wherry and two from the farm would work together, forking on 38 to 40 tons of beet, and they had no time to waste. The total weight of the loaded wherry was about 70 to 80 tons and if she was not out of the dyke and into the middle of the river before low tide she'd be sitting on the bottom.

Blucher Thain had worked with sails but by the time Eric joined him the wherry was pushed along by a seven horsepower engine. Sometimes they worked at night, depending on the tide, but darkness made no difference. *'I'd been up and down the river so much I knew it with my eyes shut. The thing I didn't like was fog. I remember coming across Breydon in the fog when the water was low and suddenly we saw a coaster of about 700 or 800 tons that had been up to Norwich. That was really frightening!'*

At the end of the season the staithe would be covered with three feet of mud, or more, but the wherry owners soon cleaned that up. It was the best topsoil, fallen from the beet, and in great demand by the owners of the bungalows on the rond, to make up their gardens and lawns. In the summertime the wherries were hired by drainage contractors to cart mud cleaned from the broad and build up the banks.

Until the last war life largely revolved around the traditional farming year. There were about fifteen farms within the village, all with their typical cluster of red brick buildings, barns, stables, cart sheds and cowsheds, either thatched or roofed with Norfolk pantiles. The names are attractive; Charity (Heigham) Farm, Cherry Tree, Marsh Farm, Hall Farm, Myrtle, Bethel Farm and Dovehouse, Cherry Garden, two called Rose Farm, The Homestead and Bowers, which was named after its one time owner. Now only Rookery Farm is still a working farm with its house and outbuildings intact.

In those days a man could get a living and raise a family on 20 acres. If he had 30 acres that was a really good living and he would probably employ a man or a boy. Life was simple, but it was the same for everyone. *'We were all poor together'* is often said, and that fact takes away any bitterness. Almost all say they were happy.

His round finished, Ivan Stimpson stops for a chat at Bethel Farm. (Photo: Hilda Stimpson)

Old Post Office, Station Road.

Harvest at Rookery Farm, 1948. (Photo: Betty Gallaugher)

Pensioners outside the old Post Office in 1930. Standing, left fo right-William 'Chips' George, carpenter; Paddy Brooks, shoemaker; John Durrant, farm worker; George Flatt, railway worker; William Goodwin, fisherman; his blind son Walter. Seated-Robert 'Hodger' George, farm worker; Sam Pollard, shopkeeper. (Photo: Ronnie George)

A SPARROW-HOUSE

This is said to have stood just at the back of Dovehouse Farm. It was open-sided, just a thatched roof mounted on four legs, with nets hanging around, and was used to catch sparrows for making sparrow pie. Chaff and wheat were put inside as bait, the birds flew down and when a good number were inside a string could be pulled which dropped the nets, trapping the sparrows. The birds were killed and just the breasts plucked and sliced off to make the pie filling. Sparrows were also culled because of the damage they could do to thatched roofs.

FUNERALS

When anyone died it was customary to toll the bell for an hour. It was a doleful chilling sound, especially since everyone knew everyone else. *'I can hear the bell out,'* childhood memory recalls a grandmother saying. *'I wonder who's dead?'*

Samuel Grapes, carpenter and undertaker, who lived at the Limes, Station Road, made the coffins in his shop at the back of his house. He had a long trolley cart with a pony to transport the coffin to the cottage, where it would be stood on trestles, and left open for relatives and friends to look at when they visited.

On the day of the funeral the coffin would be carried to the church on the bearers' shoulders, a long way if it was from a cottage in Decoy Road. In 1925 the village bought a memorial bier. The farmers were taken for their last ride on one of their own wagons, drawn by a black or dark brown horse. Most people would turn out for a funeral procession, walking behind the coffin, and it it was someone really well known the church would be packed to overflowing.

Funeral of Mr William Balls of Rookery Farm in 1928. (Photo: Betty Gallaugher)

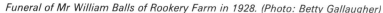

THE RAILWAY TAVERN

Old, thatched, originally just a simple beerhouse, the Tavern stood at the corner of Church Road and Station Road, and despite its name was probably there before the advent of the railway. Beer was kept in a cool flagged room, down several steps, and drawn straight from the barrel. In front of it was a small shop, where general groceries were sold. It was a popular meeting place for the men, and had a bowling green, surrounded by a hedge of sweetly scented syringa.

One regular customer always gave his horse a pint of beer when he stopped to partake of refreshment for himself. It would seem that they were a well-matched pair, equally addicted to the god Bacchus, for the horse would stop and refuse to move on until he had had his tipple.

The Railway Tavern and shop. The bowling green in the foreground. (Photo: Eileen Evans)   *The Falgate, 1907*

BOAT BUILDERS

George Applegate, the son of a local farmer, set up the first boatyard in Potter Heigham in 1895, just south of the bridge. He advertised *Yachts from three to eight tons, also open and Sailing boats for hire. Sole lessee of the celebrated "HEIGHAM SOUND" and "WHITTLESEA".'* Yachts at this time, with sleeping accommodation for four to six persons, could be hired for about £4 per week, including man. Terms for lug-sail open boats with awning, were about £1.10s (£1.50) and even at that price *'including man'*.

In 1901 The Norfolk Broads Yachting Co, latching on to the growing holiday trade, opened several boatyards, including one to the north of the old bridge. Walter Woods was manager until the company folded in 1920, when he acquired, and renamed it Walter Woods and Sons. Young Walter and Herbert were apprenticed to their father, and when old Walter died in about 1925, Herbert took over.

He expanded the business quite rapidly and moved over to the present site in 1935. He began to dig out basins there and built the first sheds. He was an innovator, largely self taught but with an eye for a good boat. He built modern holiday cruisers with streamlined shapes, smart and fast, designed in such a way that they didn't leave a lot of wash behind. The names of the boats all included the word *'light'*. The smaller cruisers were *'Delight'*, the next size *'Twilight'* and the bigger ones had such names as *'Princess of Light'* and *'Star of Light'*. The boat Herbert built for his wife was called *'Queen of Light'*. With new owners the names of many have been changed but the knowledgeable can still easily recognise a Herbert Woods boat.

Herbert Woods Yacht Station, railway line and far beyond, 1952. (Photo: Jill Grapes)   Billy May built crab boats for the Cromer men. (Photo: Billy May)

CROMER CRAB BOATS

Over a period of 25 years Billy May built 50 crab boats for the Cromer men and all are still in use except two. All are of a very special shape, able to get off the shore when it's rough. *'She must lift forward and throw the water clear, handle in rough seas, the wind mustn't blow her about too much, so she can hang on the pots, and of course, stick fairly rough weather. When they come in if it's rough, they surf ashore, at about 20 miles an hour. The bow of the boat must never dip, so if a big wave comes up behind they'll pick up with it and when they hit the beach they put the tiller hard down. There's a lot of tide running in Norfolk and the surf runs along the beach and that brings the waves in at an angle, and as soon as the boat touches the bottom, they come round into the waves. Then the men jump out and sit on the side, and the shape of the boat is very important, because she must lie over so the next wave washes her up the beach and doesn't fill her.'* One of Billy May's crab boats is on show in Cromer museum.

IN THE SECOND WORLD WAR

When war was declared all the pleasure boats from Potter Heigham were moved out of the village, either to Hickling or to Wroxham. The old bridge was mined and a Home Guard unit formed to guard it at night, even though their rifles had no bullets. The village became a restricted area, as Herbert Woods boatyard swung over to war work.

Among the craft built there were Motor Torpedo Boats, 72ft Harbour Defence Launches, 35ft pinnaces, 16ft cutters, and over sixty 32ft airborne lifeboats for the RAF. 112ft Fairmile Class Patrol boats were built for the Navy in the huge shed near the river. They filled almost the whole length of the shop. Launching them into the narrow river was difficult; the dock had to be dammed off, a slipway constructed with of rails, and when the boat hit the water it seemed as if the whole bottom of the river blew up, scattering sand and shells and mud.

The Home Guard outside the old School House. Mr Herbert Woods is seated second from the right. The photo also includes Messrs Adams, Wicks, Ives and Spurge. (Photo: Jill Grapes)

The MTBs had four American 1600 horsepower supercharged Merlin engines with four propellors. *'We couldn't use them to power the boats down river,'* said Mr Gibbs, who was in charge of the operation. *'So we had Blucher's old wherry to tow them, and it took us two days to get to Yarmouth, though there was practically no one else on the river.'* The gun turrets, torpedo tubes etc were made in the yard but fitted at a base in Yarmouth; even without the superstructure they had only about six inches headroom under Acle Bridge. The old suspension bridge was the worst hazard; with the sluice and the tide, the water could be running at about six miles an hour, they had to judge it right and shoot through. Close to 400 people worked at the boatyard during the war years, including many women whose nimble fingers developed special skills.

V E NIGHT

There was a pillbox on the corner near the Top Shop (now the post Office). One lady retains vivid memories of that area. *'We children used to play around that old pillbox and when it rained there was a foot of water in it.'* On the day the war ended the whole country celebrated, including Potter Heigham, led by their own special comedian Sidney Grapes who owned a garage in Station Road. He made sure the blackout was well and truly over as he brought out lots of old tyres, piled them on top of the pillbox and set light to them. It made a glorious bonfire that burned well into the night. What ever did Aunt Agatha say about that!

P.S. Aunt Agatha, she say, *'Other people's faults are like car headlights, they seem more glaring than your own.'*

Aunt Agatha, she say, *'If you're hard up, do without a few things our grandparents never dreamt about.'*

Aunt Agatha she say, *'It doesn't matter what happens, there's always someone who knew it would.'*

Aunt Agatha, she say, *'The cost of living is always about the same-all you've got.'*

Aunt Agatha, she say, *'It's a good thing to change your mind now and again-it keeps it clean.'*

Aunt Agatha, she say, *'You can always tell a Norfolk man. but you can't tell him much.'*

Aunt Agatha, she say, *'We are all sent here to help others.'* Granfar say, *'Well wot are the others sent for?'*

Top Shop circa 1920.

Inside back cover: The Regatta 1957
(Photo: EDP)

Back cover: High's Mill formerly Grapes 1900
(Photo: Bert High)

Some other titles in this series:

Caister — 2000 Years a Village

An Acle Chronicle

Coltishall — Heyday of a Broadland village

Have you Heard About Blakeney?

Cley — Living with Memories of Greatness

Poppyland — Strands of Norfolk History

Salthouse — Village of Character and History

Cromer — The Chronicle of a Watering Place

Great Yarmouth — History, Herrings and Holidays

Palling — A History Shaped by the Sea

Published by Poppyland Publishing, North Walsham, Norfolk.
Design by Top Floor Design.
Printed by Printing Services (Norwich) Ltd.
First edition published 1989. ISBN 0 946148 38 4

Price: £2.45